The Scientific & Religious Discoveries in the Great Pyramid

THE
Scientific and Religious Discoveries
IN THE
GREAT PYRAMID,

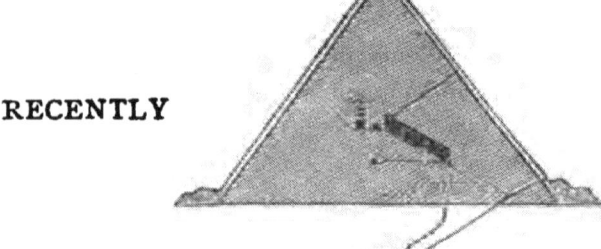

RECENTLY MADE BY

PROFESSOR PIAZZI SMYTH,

AND OTHER NOTED SCHOLARS.

Compiled By
WILLIAM H. WILSON.

CHICAGO:
F. H. REVELL, 148 & 150 MADISON STREET,
Publisher of Evangelical Literature.
1881.

PREFATORY NOTE.

We send this small work on its mission with a sincere desire that it will accomplish much good. The enemies of God's Word have labored diligently to show that the Scriptures and Science are at variance, and have overthrown the faith of some. It has been shown by students of the Great Pyramid that true science and the Holy Scriptures are in perfect accord. There is that which men call science, described by the Apostle Paul as " profane and vain babblings and oppositions of science falsely so called;" of such let us beware.   W. H. W.

EXPLANATION OF CUT ON PAGE 55.

The cut on page 55 represents a vertical section of the Great Pyramid [from north to south] showing junction of entrance passage and first ascending passage looking west.

A—shows axis of entrance, north. G—Granite Portcullis. P—Plummet Line. AD—50.3, commencing near portcullis. D G—29.8. G J—29.8. BE—32.6. EH—29.7. HK—28.8. CF—14.1. FI—30. DI—30. inches.

A TABLE OF MEASUREMENTS.

The base of the Pyramid covers 13½ square acres
The length of a base side is 9131 Pyramid inches
The vertical height is 5813 Pyramid inches, (484 feet)
Solid contents of the Pyramid 313,590 cubical fathoms
The mouth of entrance passage 50 feet above the ground
Entrance 25 feet east of the center
Doorway 47 3 high, 41.5 broad, dips at an angle 26.3 degrees
Subterranean rock chamber 100 feet below the center of the base
Subterranean chamber is 46 feet long, and 28 feet broad
Ascending passage leading from the entrance passage to the Grand Gallery, has its junction with the entrance passage at the distance of about 1,045 inches from its mouth
This passage is 47 inches in height, 41 in breadth, elevation 26 degrees
Southward up the first ascending passage to the commencement of the Grand Gallery is 1542 inches
The floor length of Grand Gallery from north beginning to its southern termination is 1881-2 inches
Height of Grand Gallery about 339 inches, or nearly 28 feet
Height of the door at the north end of Grand Gallery is 53 inches
Door at the south end leading to the ante chamber 43½ inches
From the beginning of Grand Gallery floor to the well called *Souterrain*, is 33 inches
The southern wall of Grand Gallery impends 1 degree
Length of Grand Gallery midway between floor and roof 1878.4 inches
Number of roof stones to this Gallery 36
Number of overlapping stones on the side walls 7
Cubical contents of Grand Gallery 36,000,000 inches
Strange exit from the upper corner of Grand Gallery 28 feet above floor
Length of short passage leading from the Grand Gallery to the antechamber is 52.19 inches
Length of ante-chamber 116.26
Breadth from east to west 65 inches
The height 149 inches
Wall of passage way between ante and King's Chambers 100 inches thick
The King's Chamber is 412 in length, 206 in breadth, 230 in height
King's Chamber shielded from outside heat or cold by 180 feet masonry
Temperature of King's Chamber 50 degrees
From base of Pyramid to King's Chamber 50 courses of masonry
Wall courses of granite in King's chamber 5
First 4 courses 4 feet high, 5th and lower one sinks one-tenth below floor
Outside measurement of Coffer in King's Chamber, length: 89.62 depth, 41.13, breadth, 38.61.

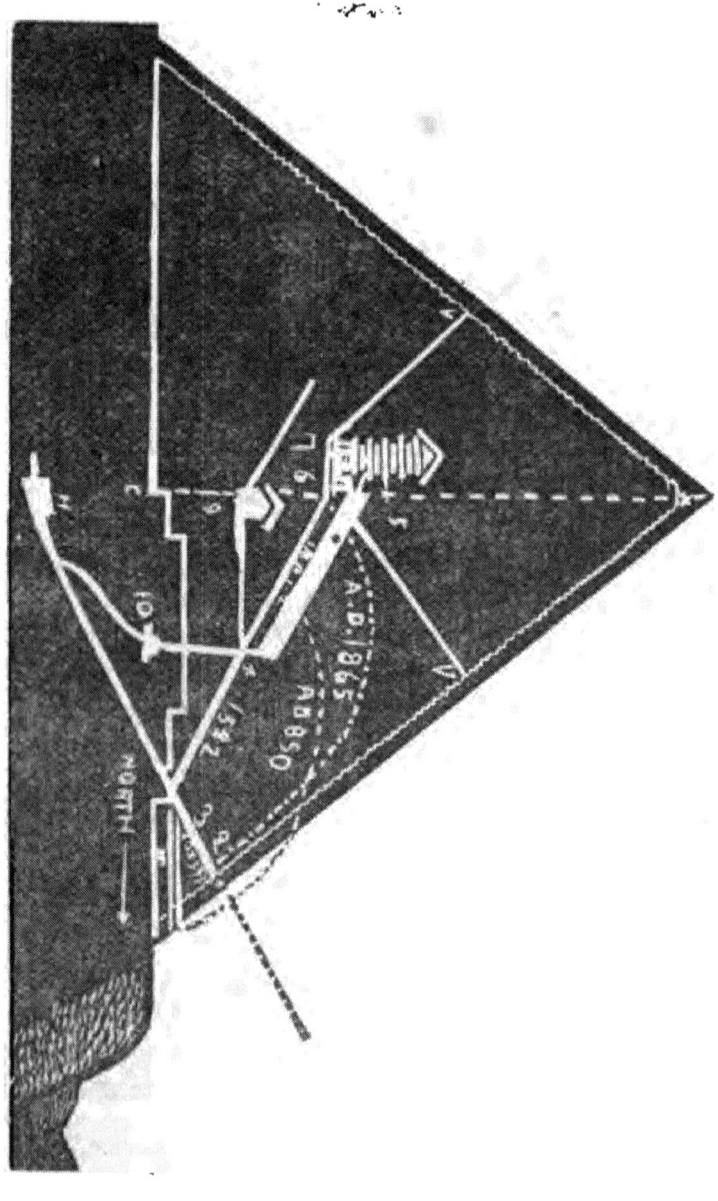

V V—Air Passages. H—Subterranean Chamber. C M—Base Side. 2, 3—Descending Passage. 4—First Ascending Passage and entrance to Grand Gallery. 6—Ante-Chamber. 7—Coffer. King's Chamber over 7, 6. 9—Queen's. 10—Souterrain. A—Draconis, Pole Star.

CHAPTER I.

The Pyramid's Antiquity and Greatness.

All the ordinary hieroglyphics, and papyrus-rolls, and mummy remains by which Egypt is now generally known throughout the world, and by their means understood to have been a powerful monarchy long before either Homer sang or Troy fell—all these things are very modern compared with the Great Pyramid. In fact, our only resource and only method of obtaining understandable landmarks of reference for such exceedingly early times is to appeal to the most ancient and best of all books, and tell you from its sacred pages that this Great Pyramid was enabled to date from before Joseph and Jacob, and Isaac, and even Abraham; nay, it even goes close up to the time of the dispersion of the human race on the plains of Shinar. In stating this, I am far within the generality of dates which have been recently applied to the Great Pyramid by classical, philological, and hieroglyphic scholars; yet, if within, it is not that we fear to state to you the whole truth, whatever that might be; but it is because the Great Pyramid itself under the latest application to it of practical astronomical science, seems to tell its own date of birth and foundation. And that date—while it most fully justifies the near parallelism already alluded to with the dispersion on the plains of

Shinar—yet by no means supports the dates of those very learned, literary, metaphysical, and generally unscientific gentlemen who aver that the Great Pyramid is not only founded in ages and at dates that would place it before the Deluge, but before the creation of Adam as well. A little more than four thousand years, then, is the full length of past existence we claim for the Great Pyramid. If it be asked how the stones of the Pyramid can have lasted in any finished and intelligible form so long, we reply that here (in our island home—Scotland) frost and rain are the chief agents in the destruction of stone, but in the dry and sultry climate of Egypt so exceedingly slight is the pure decay which takes place in earthy matter, that even crude or unbaked bricks, formed merely of Nile mud, have been known to last some three thousand years; and stone blocks, of which Egypt has vast supplies and of excellent quality, have lasted longer still.

It appears, however, from hieroglyphic inscriptions, first interpreted in the present century, and corroborated by traditions and some historic records, that the great Egyptian pyramid was erected three or four hundred years before the time of Abraham, and eight or nine hundred years before the era of Moses. It is a gigantic structure. The perpendicular height is about 480 feet. This huge fabric consists of two hundred and six layers of vast blocks of stone, rising above each other in the form of steps, the thickness of which diminishes as the height increases, the lower layers being nearly five feet in thickness, and the upper ones about eighteen inches. The summit of the pyramid appears to have been, originally, a level platform, sixteen or eighteen feet square. Herodotus states that one hundred thousand men were employed twenty years in its construction, and that ten years had been spent previously in quarrying the stones and conveying them to the place.

With Greeks, Romans, Arabs, and modern Europeans, the Pyramid has ever been an increasing source of wonder and speculation. Conquerors—from Cambyses the Persian down to Napoleon Bonaparte—have essayed, but in vain, to penetrate its secret; nor have the endeavors of philosophers been wanting; and the more the questions relating to the reasons for its construction were pushed, the more distant did the answer appear. It is only within the last very few years that the veil of the mystery has begun to be lifted.

The first movement in this direction was in 1859, when the late John Taylor of London, discovered how fraught with mathematical and physical meaning is the peculiar angle at which are built the sides of the Great Pyramid, and of the Great Pyramid alone of all pyramids throughout both Egypt and the whole world. The next step was the discovery, by him also, that the Great Pyramid memorialized a very remarkable standard of length. Scientifically, it is founded on the best possible feature of nature-reference ever thought of by men, and is a most convenient fraction thereof, for it is exactly the one-ten-millionth of the earth's semi-axis of rotation. And while in its whole length it is found to be identical also with the sacred cubit of the Hebrews—before they went down into Egypt, as well as afterward—in its subdivisions it represents the inches of Anglo-Saxon and most of the Gothic descended nations. Then followed the discovery of standards of weight and capacity measure, based in similarly noble and universal earth-manner; or, in this case, on the size, combined with the mean specific-gravity of the earth as a whole; and they are likewise at the root of the weight and capacity measures both of the sacred Hebrew system and of those of the Gothic nations of Europe. Next a heat standard, based on the mean temperature of the whole surface of the earth; and marks boiling water at 250°; the greatest density of water, at 10°; and the freezing of water at 0°. An angular measure founded on a decimal treatment of the circle. And, lastly, a time measure, not only recording the week of seven days and the sabbatic week, but giving a method of chronology capable of fixing the date of the Pyramid to exceeding exactness. Showing it, too, to have been erected so many centuries before Moses, that that circumstance, taken in connection with the sabbatic record just mentioned, appears to overthrow for ever the writings of all those of the fathers, who, from the times of Irenæus and Justin Martyr, down to some men still living, have endeavored to establish the belief that the Sabbath was never heard of in the world until Moses taught it to the Israelites at Sinai.

All these remarkable interpretations of what the very stones of the Great Pyramid seem to be calling out to those who are enabled to hear, were not arrived at without many minds being brought to bear on the question, and pursuing it steadily, seriously, and anxiously, year after year. But even their labors were not very fruitful, nor all their conclusions sound, until new, improved, and more accurate measures of the Pyramid were recently procured.

Professor C. Piazzi Smyth, Astronomer Royal of Scotland, says: "The Great Pyramid is the highest and holiest subject that can ever occupy a scientific society, supposed now, under an increased body of evidence, to have been erected under the eye of Melchizedek, and according to a design furnished by Divine inspiration. The last seventeen years, (and no more) have, strange to say, shown to the eye of modern science, a most grand, ancient, solid, and mysterious building, accurately fulfilling on the most crucial examination everything that has been stipulated for, and even in a manner to make the wisest among us draw their breath in awe."

The Great Pyramid stands in latitude 30°, at the center of an arc which sweeps the Delta of lower Egypt. Its base covers over thirteen square acres, and is built upon a rock leveled for the purpose. The four corner stones are let into the main rock, and the four sides of the building face exactly the four cardinal points of the heavens.

If indeed the great Builder of the earth itself has caused to be reared a structure of such vastness and durability as the Great Pyramid, and that for the special advantage of His people in the grand crisis of this closing dispensation—reared it for a testimony to His truth and foresight, and to bridge the chasm of ages, how willing and thankful we should be to meditate the testimony. When scientific reasonings are arrayed in objection to revelation, how assuring to behold in the Pyramid an irrefutable proof of the truth and power of God's intervention in human affairs, in such a manner as to confirm the Mosaic record. Science and revelation are linked together in this grand pillar. That God who is the Author of all the wonders that exercise the scientist, all of the atoms and elements in Nature, and the laws that establish and control their relations; that He is also the God of Abraham and Moses and Melchizedek, this is what we delight to behold in the Pyramid.

The Great Pyramid is really a most gigantic proof that that eventful beginning of stone architecture, by the highest and best built structure that has ever yet been erected, shows that Divine inspiration must have energized its builders.

The Great Pyramid scholars attest the truth of the Noachic deluge, the dispersion of mankind from Babel, together with the miracle of the erection of the ancient Great Pyramid in the manner which sets at naught all worldly wisdom to explain, but with regard to which the inspired Word said long ago, speaking in the name of God, "I have declared, the former things from the beginning, they went forth out of my mouth, and I showed them; I did them suddenly, and they came to pass" (Isa. xlviii. 3). In short, after modern science had been allowed by the Almighty to wax strong in the world, and has, like Jeshurun, grown fat, and kicked against Biblical authority, declaring on its own fiat alone, that a miracle is impossible, lo, that very modern science is involuntarily the chief agent, in proving by the contemporary Great Pyramid, that a miracle did once occur, in the early history of mankind; and if we live in times when this unexpected but clearly-proved discovery has been made, may it not be to warn us of the time near approaching, when miraculous interference will again take place on the surface of the earth, for the accomplishment of the mysteries of God?

It is understood by many eminent Biblical scholars that

special reference is made to the Great Pyramid in Isa. xix. 19, which reads as follows : "In that day shall there be an altar to the Lord in the midst of the land of Egypt, and a pillar at the border thereof to the Lord; and it shall be for a sign and for a witness unto the Lord of hosts in the Land of Egypt." At first sight there arises a peculiar difficulty in the Scripture just quoted from Isaiah, inasmuch as it requires apparently a solid stone monument to be in two places at once : that is, " in the midst of the land of Egypt," and also " at the border thereof."

The apparent opposition of these verbal terms is at once relieved by looking to the peculiar physical geography of lower Egypt. This remarkable explanation was produced only a few years ago, when Mr. Henry Mitchel, Chief Hydrographer of the United States Survey, being sent to report on the Suez Canal, found the northern coast line of all lower Egypt such a striking example of a sectoral or fan-shaped form from a center, that he proceeded to ascertain by measures from the curved outer coast, and the radial branching streams of the Nile in the Delta, the necessary position of that remarkable central point, and he found it to be on the northern edge of the Pyramid hill of Jeezeh. Now all men knew long ago, that the Great Pyramid was built just on the brink of the desert outside of Egypt, or "on the border thereof," and in that case it could not be also in the midst or center of it, as centers are usually understood. But the now ascertained shape of that country as a sector removes the difficulty, for a sector's center is necessarily and mathematically in one extreme corner of its area. The Great Pyramid then does in this case satisfy the demands of prophecy respecting the location in the midst of the land of Egypt, while it is found on careful calculation to be in the center not only, but in the middle also of all the dry, inhabitable land surface of the whole world. Hence, if there ever is to be on this globe a monument central to all mankind, an almost necessary condition for a metrological [for weights and measures] monument to all nations, the Great Pyramid already stands on that spot, and has stood there through all human history, and is gifted with special qualifications to act as that building.

Now such a site could not have been *intentionally* selected by any, even of the most learned schoolmen among the ancients, for they could know nothing of the existence of America, Australia, and other large regions which are necessary to be taken into calculation. Hence, the *intention* did not preside ; it could be the result only of Divine inspiration imparted to certain men. And here we have the explanation of a puzzling feature in Josephus' narrative touching the sons of Seth, that when these righteous, hard-working men proposed to monumentalize the scientific and astronomical discoveries, previously made by Divine assistance, they did not erect the monument in Chaldea or Palestine, where the observations were made, but went down into [of all discreditable places for such men,] the Cainite land of Sirad of Egypt, the reason being because there only was the requisite geographical center for a monument, which, in the latter day was to have a message, a meaning, and a use for all the nations of the world.

An old Coptic tradition declares, says Prof. Smyth, that to annihilate the Great Pyramid would more than consume all the wealth of Egypt. It is worthy of notice that no mutilation or loss which it has sustained has been such as to baffle science in accurately determining its measures. Its fiducial points are, in our day, all recoverable, so that its witness-bearing shall be faithful and plain. How eminently becoming the truth-seeking mind to cherish its teachings, even though Catholics will have nothing to do with an institution older than their own church. Nor should we be one of that class of Protestants who think themselves bound to oppose the very first mention of anything good in the Great Pyramid, because it stands in *Egypt*, on the ground that it is or must be wholly Egyptian and Pharaonic, and therefore to be held by all Christian men as profane, vile, Cainite, and altogether abominable, since of Christ Himself it is said, "Out of Egypt have I called my Son," and the Lord of hosts shall say, "Blessed be Egypt my people, and Assyria the work of mine hands, and Israel mine inheritance."

The eastern escarpment of the pyramid hill shows limestone, with a southeastern dip. In the rocky bulk of the pyramid hill, out of which much of the building material was excavated, nummulites abound, about the size of a pea, and called Strabo's beans, sometimes cunningly sold as curiosities by Arab boys to travelers, who soon afterwards find them by thousands. The yellowish stone from pyramid hill was largely used for the construction of tombs, which abound in the vicinity. On the east and south surface of the hill the tombs are sometimes square wells twenty, fifty and seventy-five feet deep.

The rocky surface underneath the pyramid is to a considerable extent an artificially leveled area. At the northeast corner the lowest course and part of another is natural rock, and again in the entrance passage, a little below Al Mamoon's hole, and again in the course of the well twenty or thirty feet above the pyramid base. One writer speaks of the pyramid as "built on two hills." The cubic contents of this enormous structure are more than eighty millions of cubic feet, and the material of which it is composed would serve to build a stone wall five feet high and one foot thick, of a greater length than three thousand miles. Let us suppose that taking the population together, it would require seven persons, men, women and children, to move a ton in weight; then accepting the pyramid's estimated weight at six millions of tons, it would require forty-two millions of persons, or the entire population of the United States, to move the Great Pyramid, rolling on twenty-four millions of wheels; or sixty thousand steam engines would be required, drawing each one hundred tons. The stones are generally seven or eight feet in length and breadth, and four or five feet thick. In the temple wall at Jerusalem, they were nineteen or twenty feet long, and at Baalbec more than sixty.

Diodorus Siculus says the chief wonder about the practical building of the Great Pyramid is, "What became of the pieces? There is no vestige, not the smallest trace of the chippings in stone, so that the whole building seems as if placed on the surrounding sand by aid of some Deity, rather than by the sole and gradual operations of man."

But the mystery of the fragments is explained, for sudden torrents from storms show one-half of the northern hill to be pyramid chips, and beyond a short distance ravines from sixty to seventy feet deep are cut in them. Vyse mentions holes in the rock northeast of the pyramid, near the northern causeway, for rows of lifting machines. Perring found round holes in the pyramid for the same purpose. Near the top of the heap are chips of black and white diorite, much the same as the statue of Shafre, in Boolak. No such material is seen in any tomb, or in the pyramid itself, except near the entrance passage. Hence the inference of an undiscovered room in the pyramid—the muniment room for the monument. Multitudes have hewed and hacked to find it. When or how it **may be discovered, or what it may reveal, who can tell?**

CHAPTER II.

Preparatory Work.

Before entering upon a detailed description of the measurements of the different passages, gallery, chambers, etc., of this mighty structure, it may be of interest and profit to refer briefly to some portions of the preparatory work of Prof. Smyth, previous to his engaging in the scientific investigations of this ancient building, and also to relate some points of interest connected with the Pyramid, which, if borne in mind by the reader, will enable him to more clearly comprehend that which is to follow.

The work of making preparation for the expedition was no slight undertaking. There were many obstacles to overcome, such as required a man of science and forethought to foresee and provide for. His outfit consisted of eight camel-loads of boxes, which contained no less than twenty-seven boxes of instruments. All things being ready, Prof. Smyth and wife left Edinburg, Scotland, in November 1864, and in due time arrived at Egypt, and soon after engaged in the work before them. The Professor was assisted in his work by Ismail Basha, Viceroy of Egypt; by Mariette Bey, Superintendent of Monuments; by Zeki Bey, Master of Ceremonies, and by Signor Vassalis, Superintendent of excavations, and Governor of Jeezeh. Other helpers are also mentioned, including Andrew Coventry, of Edinburgh, who furnished money for the purchase of two excellent measuring instruments for the angular inclination, and linear height of the Grand Gallery. The American Missionary furnished him with a good and faithful servant, named Ibraheem. Mr. Vassalis brought two reis or captains, and twenty men from Sakkara, to be employed in cleaning pyramid passages, and washing down the floors and walls, preparatory to the work in anticipation. There was a necessity to begin immediately, because the Mohammedan fast of Ramadan would commence in three weeks, and then the men would be disabled from work by weakness. Boxes were unpacked, and candles and candlesticks taken out, and two Sakkara boys and Allee Dobree accompanied them to the pyramid.

Meanwhile, Reis Alee Shafei commenced, through his Sakkara men and boys, to sweep the chambers and passages, calling often for candles, lamps, lucifers, brooms, etc. The clouds of dust in sweeping the passages were fearful. Cleaning utensils were also extemporized by Mr. S., and the work prosecuted successfully. Reis Allee Shafei reports large blocks of stone at the bottom, or lower end of the entrance passage, which were taken out of Al Mamoon's forced hole [an opening made several hundred years ago, at a point not far from the real opening, then unknown, and intersecting, accidentally, with the entrance passage]. M. Vassalis will not permit the stones to be broken preparatory to removal, without first consulting Mariette·Bey. At length the work of cleaning was completed, the men paid, and dismissed in time for the fast of Ramadan.

CHAPTER III.

Measurements and what they Signify.

The entrance is on the north side, and fifty feet above the base, and twenty-five feet east of the center of the pyramid. The stone courses around the entrance are of a whiter, denser stone than the others, and slightly, curiously, and exactly inclined from a right angle. The floor is much harder than the walls or roof, and extends further out, the latter being partly broken for some distance inwards. The doorway is 47.3 inches high, and 41.5 inches wide, and dips at an angle of 26.3°. There were shallow notches in the floor across the stones every two or three feet, and increasing in depth and frequency. At the bottom of the descending passage, or its intersection with the ascending, was a steep bank of sand, placed there by Arabs to avoid the trouble of escorting travelers along the continuation of the passage downwards for more than 200 feet to the subterranean chamber, which is the largest in the pyramid. There is a large cavernous hole opening sidewise from the west wall above the sand bank. Then facing south and scaling a small cliff by small holes in the stones for the fingers, and turning west, the ascending passage is reached above the portcullis stop. The ascending passage rises at an angle of 26.3°. There are notches in the floor, made in comparatively recent times, to assist in climbing, and the roof and walls are rounded and cavernous.

At the right is a square hole, by a short duct leading to the well. Here commences the horizontal floor of the passage leading south to the queen's chamber. There are ramps along the sides of the Grand Gallery, sometimes missing and the holes filled with dust. Seven overlappings of stone tables are seen in the walls, with fractures from their edges. There is a step three feet high at the upper end.

Thence we enter, by a low passage southward, into the granite constructions. Another stoop and then comes the king's chamber. The coffer is at the western end. In the northwest corner is a long hole, caused by undermining to find mummy-pits in the limestone masonry. The floor stones were once equisitely jointed.

Five hollow chambers of construction are built in over the ceiling, to prevent too great pressure from the enormous superincumbent mass above. The ante-chamber is 116.26 inches in length, and if this number be multiplied by the quantity, which the best of modern science has computed to be the particular fractional number for squaring the circle, viz., the proportion of the length of the diameter to the length of a circumference of a circle or 3.14156, the result is 365,24, or the number of solar days and parts of a day contained in a solar tropical year, as ascertained by modern astronomy, very exactly, but always blundered at by ancient astronomers, even 2000 years after the day of the Great Pyramid.

The coffer in the king's chamber is of exactly similar cubical capacity with the ark of the covenant, and con-

structed long before the ark, and placed in the pyramid's heart, and built in so as never to be removed. The west side of the coffer was found to be slightly the lowest, with grooves cut in three other sides, and pin-holes, apparently for the lid. A lump of limestone was found in the coffer, for the use of travelers in breaking off fragments for mementos, which was taken away. The room was extremely dusty, and the air chambers chocked.

The joints of masonry work within are wonderfully fine and straight. No modern optical instrument maker could work better straight-edges, even after 4000 years of expansion, contraction, lightning and earthquake. In the main portion of the pyramid the breadth of the joints is often measurable by inches, being filled full of coarse, pinkish mortar, yet substantial, and arranged so as to break joints scrupulously. But in the beginning of the entrance passage the joints are cemented with fine white cement, almost microscopically thin, showing great skill, trouble and expense. The floor is measured in inches and tenths of an inch, from joint to joint, the character of each joint being noted, and the quality of stone. The inclination is ten degrees greater than what is called the angle of repose for wood or stone. The floor blocks are much the hardest, and the best joints are near the two ends of the passage. The stones are of unlike size, but break joints well, the object being a certain angle without great expense or ornament.

Prof. Smyth discovers a line on either wall, ruled, apparently, by a masterly hand, as a guide to the original working masons. Compared with this, the *mean* of all the errors was zero, or nothing. Seven or eight feet of the lower floor are as hard as flint and tough as slate, and from this extra hardness have effectually defied both time and hammers. There are three stones with two oblique joints, which are two secret key-marks [designed for men in a remote period], and *vis a vis* to the lower butt end of the portcullis block, closing the entrance to all the *ascending* passages of the pyramid, under the stone space where Al Mamoon's workmen heard a falling sound. Here, behind these joints lay a concealed entrance to the secret, internal constructions of the pyramid. The unfinished subterranean chamber, cut far down beneath the pyramid's base, reached by a passage continuing from the descending entrance passage, was designed for a blind.

The Grand Gallery floor is a continuation of the floor of the former passage, with the same breadth and the same southern direction. A horizontal passage goes under the elevated floor of the Grand Gallery, a *cul de sae*, and not considered a part of the show for travelers. In this passage and chamber there is no floorway of white Mokattam stone, but ordinary masonry courses, and on two different levels. The walls are lined with the finest and purest stone of all, whiter, closer, more polishable and exquisitely planed, with the closest joints of microscopic exactness. Cement was used to ensure durability, and to prevent depredations of intruders.

Howard Vyse settled the question as to whether the pyramid was cased, for in digging down on the north face, he found two huge casing stones and part of a third *in situ*, and held by cement, the material being hard white Mokattam stone. The rubbish heaps, apical in shape, except on the north side, evidently came from the pyramid, being the same in color, a yellow ochry crust, two or three feet deep, but underneath are fragments of white limestone only. Prof. Smyth particularly wanted a stone where two surfaces met together. At last Alec Dobree found one [and more were afterward found] with an angle of 128°, showing that it was fitted to the angular inclination of about 52° of Pyramid sides. The outside surface was like bright painted brown walnut wood; the interior sides were white, with traces of white cement, and in smoothness far exceeding the chisel work of our day. These specimens were probably knocked off to suit the rectangular masonry of new buildings, in the construction of which they were employed. The rubbish heaps on the east, west and south sides were never explored.

The Great Pyramid's very first pure mathematical problem, ascertained by the late John Taylor in 1859, is that celebrated one in modern times of the most practical mode of squaring the circle, i. e., ascertaining very closely the proportion of length between the diameter and circumference of a circle, and it is accomplished at the Great Pyramid by giving its sides such a particular angle of slope that the vertical axis shall bear to two sides of the base the proportion of 1 to 3.14159. The angle of slope of the sides is 51°, 51', and 43.3". It is easy to see that a very slight variation in the angle of slope will affect the height either to augment or diminish it. But with this exact angle, we have a height of 5813 Pyramid inches, or 5819 English inches.

We do not give these lengths to a minutely fractional exactness. Of course, the ratio between the height and the sum of two sides, being as above intimated, the height becomes the radius of a circle whose circumference is equal to the sum of four sides, and the area of a right section is in the same ratio of the base. Now, *why* or *how* was this exact angle given to the sides? Was it a mere accident, a strange coincidence? A variation of one degree, or even one-half a degree, would have rendered this ratio of course impossible. Are mathematical truths evolved by accident or would such a truth be accidentally expressed in the erection of such a monument? If by the merest chance *one* such expression were lodged in eighty million cubic feet of masonry, how enormously would the chances multiply against the embodiment of a second and third mathematical problem. Yet there are more than three, or three times three important scientific truths in the Great Pyramid.

This building's first astronomic problem was discovered by Wm. Petrie in 1867, determining the sun's distance from the earth. This was represented at the Pyramid 4000 years ago by its chief line of measure, or its central vertical height, when multiplied by the numbers which its shape typifies, to wit: 10 raised to the 9th power. In other words 5819 English inches multiplied by 1,000,000,000=91,840,000 miles nearly. No other building, not even St. Peter's at Rome, or the Strasburg Cathedral, has ever attained such a height as the Pyramid.

A peculiar relation exists between the sun's mean distance, the size of the earth, the number of days in a year, and the proportion of the Great Pyramid. What is that relation? The length of a base side of this pyramid, [and not in another pyramid in Egypt] is such that when divided by the number of days in a year, that is 365.242, the result is to develop not only a convenient measuring rod, but one with the inestimable recommendation of being exactly the ten-millionth of the straight distance from the earth's center to either pole, or of the semi-axis of the earth's diurnal rotation in the course of its annual revolution around the sun. And this, says Prof. Smyth, makes so pre-eminently proper a nature-reference to scientific linear measure, that one of the latest and ablest of American pro-French metric writers, President Barnard, of Columbia College, New York, recently acknowledged that if the French metrical system had now to be created anew, its promoters would profit by what is now known.

The French metre rod is the ten-millionth of a curved terrestrial meridian quadrant, or one ten-millionth the distance from the equator to the pole along the earth's circumference, and is 39.3685 English inches. The French academicians who took their unit of measure in the metre, a little over eighty years ago, would now take, according to Prof. Barnard, the same fraction, that is the ten-millionth of the straight, the central line of the semi-axis of rotation of the earth. And this actually was done far earlier in the history of the world, at the building of the Great Pyramid, by the sons of Seth.

Hence, nothing better in science can be imagined, even to the masters of science, than the Great Pyramid's base side standard for a unit of measure in the sacred cubit of 25 pyramid inches. If we divide 9131, the number of inches in length of a base side by 365.242, we have, as a result, the 25 inches of the sacred cubit. And that length is quite diverse from 20.7 inch cubit of profane Egypt, Babylon, and other

Cainite lands of antiquity, while it is entirely agreeable to Sir Isaac Newton's determination of the limits within which the sacred cubit of the Hebrews would be found. And this is the cubit which Moses told his people was the cubit of the Lord their God, according to the admonition, "See that thou make all things according to the pattern showed to thee in the mount." There seems to be a reference to this cubit in Ezek. xliii. 13, where it is said, " The cubit is a cubit and a hand breadth," and again in 2 Chron. iii. 3, where it is said in reference to the dimensions of Solomon's temple, "The length by cubits after the first measure, was threescore cubits."

Be it remembered, therefore, that the earth's all-important axis of rotation measures just 500,000,000 of pyramid inches, fives and tens being the basis of the Pyramid's system of numeration, for there are that number of corners and sides. Thus the Great Pyramid's cubit is a wonderful measuring rod, and the Pyramid itself is remarkably commensurate with the sacred cubit on the one hand, and astronomically with the earth itself on the other, with an accuracy never yet attained by any other existing stone building, or work of man anywhere. This cubit was brought into Egypt at the building of the Great Pyramid, monumentalized there in stone before the visit of Abraham, and its original taken back by the owners into Palestine.

The same standard was again brought into Egypt by the children of Israel, but carefully taken out with them at the Exodus, and exclusively used by them in the preparation of the ark of the covenant, and other sacred vessels, in the wilderness. Again, for the third time, it was brought before the world, though with variations, when the Goths and Saxons appeared in the west of Europe.

We have thus two factors, the inches in a cubit, and the days in a year, and these multiplied together give the length of a pyramid base side exactly. Is this an accident? Impossible.

A little within the ante-chamber, begin the granite constructions of the pyramid, every stone outside and in, hitherto seen, except the portcullis blocks at the beginning of the first ascending passage, being limestone. Mr. Smyth was two or three days measuring and re-measuring the ante-chamber, with the help of a ladder. We defer a minute description, only remarking that it is entered by a low opening, from the Gallery, and that a granite leaf is found on the east side, 43 inches from the floor and roof, and cemented with pure white cement. It is formed in two pieces. On the upper piece is alto-relievo sculpture, one inch thick and semi-circular in shape, 7×7 inches in diameter at the inner outline, and 5×5 at the outer surface. It looks like a handle to lift the upper half and perhaps disclose a hollow space, with the key of the Pyramid. This chamber is 116 Pyramid inches in length, 65 inches in breadth from east to west, and 149 inches in height. The south granite wall of the ante-chamber is 120 inches in thickness, with a passage to the King's Chamber 43 inches in height.

The ante-chamber is 41.5 broad, and 116.26 inches long. And there is this peculiarity about the length, that part of it is in granite, and part in limestone, and the granite portion is in length 103.033 pyramid inches. Now if we multiply this last number by 50, the course of masonry on which the chamber stands, reckoning upward from the base, we have 5151.5 inches, or the length of the side of a square which is exactly equal in area to a direct vertical section of the Great Pyramid, or to a circle having the vertical section of the pyramid for a diameter, exhibiting in fact, another form of the problem of squaring the circle, which the ancient idolatrous nations knew next to nothing about.

Again, if the above number of of 116.26 inches be multiplied by 50, the result is 5813 pyramid inches, or the ancient vertical height of the Great Pyramid, as derived from the mean of all the measures of it. But can any reason be assigned for these exact measures of 116.26 and 103.33, exact to a fraction, even in thousandths, neither less nor more by a hair's breadth? The reason is obvious in the forethought of the Divine author, and not in any blind and senseless philosophy of chance, nor in any conjectured ingenuity of the uninstructed Egyptians of those days.

In the King's Chamber a beginning was made by measuring the stone floor joints. There are four straight horizontal stone joint courses and five equal stone courses in the wall spaces from the floor to the roof, with needle-proof closeness of the joints. Each course is 45 inches high, except the lowest, which is only 42 inches above the floor. The principle of 5s is a grand tendency in the Pyramid, and is carried out even in the temperature; that is, one-fifth the distance between the freezing and boiling points of water above the former. The temperature of the King's Chamber is 50°, which is the mean temperature both of all lands inhabited by man, and the most suitable degree to man. A temperature *below* which human nature seeks methods of warming, and *above* which it seeks methods of cooling, and is also the most suitable for work or play, prayer or praise, and all the accuracies of science. This Chamber is shielded from the outside heat and cold, by a thickness of nowhere less than 180 feet of solid masonry.

The size of the King's Chamber, in Pyramid inches, is 230 in height, 206 in breadth, and 412.132 in length. And why is it that length? Apparently no one had ever thought of that, until in July, 1873, Prof. Smyth, guided by a previous kindred discovery of Capt. Tracey, in the ante-chamber, ascertained that pyramid *inches* in the King's Chamber stand for pyramid *cubits* outside the Great Pyramid. Now this quantity above mentioned, that is, 412.132 as the diameter of a circle, represents accurately in area a square one side of which equals 365.242, or the number of days in a year, or the number of cubits in a base side of the pyramid. And that number again, that is, 412.132 represents in area a circle the radius of which equals the height of the pyramid, in cubits, or 232.52 cubits.

The division into five of the wall-courses of the King's Chamber of granite, sized to an equal height, strikes the eye of the traveler, as he enters the low doorway into that magnificently finished room, which is equal to fine jewelry polish. Each course round the room is about four feet in height, except the lowest course which sinks one-tenth below the floor, so that the top of the lowest course is on a level with the top of the granite coffer. Two separate sets of measured numbers in Pyramid inches, for the length, breadth and height of the lowest course, give, when divided by the coffer's contents, 50. So we have the multiple of $5+5=25$, and twice $25=50$. Now 50 is a prophetic or Jubilee number; and it is somewhat striking that the King's Chamber stands on the 50th course of masonry from the Pyramid's base, whereon also stands the granite coffer, a vessel with commensurable capacity proportions between the inside and out, and wall and floor in a room with 5 courses composed of 100 stones, and with a capacity proportion of 50 to the 5 of these courses. It is a peculiar feature of the coffer that the cubic capacity of the outside is twice that of the inside, and the number of cubic pyramid inches is nearly 71.250. And this 71.250 inches comprise the same cubic capacity with the ark of the covenant. Is this accidental? It may serve the purpose of incredulous persons to call this coincidence a mere fortuitous circumstance, but it cannot disturb the conviction of God-fearing men, that His hand formed, or caused to be formed, this wonderful pyramidal vessel. Its fourth part also represents the old Saxon measure called a "quarter," while again its typical division into 5 times 500 parts produces a standard unit of pyramid capacity, practically equal to the old British wine pint, equal in weight to the British pound also. These 2,500 pounds form also the pyramid ton, coming between the avoirdupois and shipping ton.

Fifty pyramid inches form the one ten-millionth of the earth's axis of rotation, and consequently the one ten-millionth of the semi-axis is 25 pyramid inches, the exact length, as already stated, of the sacred cubit. So we see that the King's Chamber is the standard of 50, or of two cubits length; while the Queen's Chamber is the standard of 25, or one cubit length, for it stands on the 25th course of masonry composing the pyramid. The passage which enters the Queen's Chamber is a horizontal one, leading from near the lower end of the Grand Gallery. The one grand architectural feature of the Queen's Chamber is the niche in the east wall, which symbolizes by its amount of eccentric displacement in the room, just one cubit.

We might expect to find that one ten-millions of cubic inches are indicated by this room's contents, as against the two ten-millions of the King's Chamber, which is almost exactly the case.

Both the Molten Sea of Solomon's Temple, and the Ark of the Covenant was what science in that day could not possibly have devised, that is to have made them earth commensurable. The Molten Sea contained 2,000 baths, or 50 times as much as the laver, and also exactly 50 times as much as the internal cubic contents of the sacred Ark of Moses.

It is remarkable that the lower course of the King's Chamber has been so adjusted in height, by the removal from sight of its lower 5 inches, that the cubic contents of that lower course amount to fifty times the coffer's contents, and exactly equals the cubic contents, of Solomon's Molten Sea.

"Whence, then," asks the Astronomer Royal, "came the metrological ideas common to three individuals in three different ages; and involving reference to deep cosmical attributes of the earth, understood by the best and highest of human learning at none of those times? The answer can hardly be other than that the God of Israel, who liveth forever, equally inspired the Seth-descended architect of the Great Pyramid, the prophet Moses, and King Solomon.

In the year 2170 the pole-star Draconis, was 3° and 42' from the pole of the sky, and therefore looked right down the entrance-passage, when at its lowest culmination. When the pole-star was so looking down the entrance-passage. Tauri the chief star in the Pleiades group was crossing the local terrestrial meridian, at a point high up in the sky, near the equator, and simultaneously with the celestial meridian of the vernal equinox. Modern astronomy teacher that these phenomena could only have occurred simultaneously at or about the year 2170 B. C., and this too if viewed at midnight on the 21st of September, as representing the day of the autumnal equinox.

Now the Pleiades are found by all mankind, at the present time, to come to the meridian at midnight later in the year. The difference between that date, or the 17th of November, and the date of crossing, as above mentioned, or September 21st, is seen to be 57 days. A proportion is therefore easily constructed. As the number of days in the year to 57, so will the whole precessional period be to the age of the Pyramid, or as 365 and a fraction to 57, so are 25.827 to 4040 very nearly. So that over 4040 years have elapsed since this huge monument of stone was reared in the land of Egypt

Again, the modern astronomer may measure at midnight the angular distance of the Pleiades from the meridian. Or, he may measure the angular distance from the old pole-star from the present pole of the heavens. In either case by appropriate astronomical calculations it can be determined how long ago those stars were on the meridian. And this time agrees very nearly, if not exactly, with that before mentioned. Thus, we have something definite and tangible relative to the true age of the pyramid. We are not borne backward into pre-historic or even antediluvian antiquity. At 2170 B. C., the great structure rose from its base, certifying by the verdict of astronomy the date of its origin.

CHAPTER IV.

Pyramid's Messianic Character.

Prof. Smyth says: "In the course of the Summer of 1872, in a correspondence with Mr. Charles Casey, of Pollerton Castle, Carlow, that straight-forward and vigorous thinker considered himself called on to tell me that, while he had followed and adopted all that I had attempted as to the metrology of the Great Pyramid being of more than human scientific perfection for the age in which it was produced, yet to call it therefore Divinely inspired or sacred, seemed to be either too much or too little. 'Now,' said Mr. Casey, 'unless the Great Pyramid can be shown to be Messianic, as well as fraught with superhuman science and design, its *sacred* claim is a thing with no blood in it.'"

"It was in 1865," continues Prof. Smyth, "that a letter reached me at the Great Pyramid, transmitted with some high recommendations of its author, by that most upright knightly man, the late Mr. Maitland, Sheriff Clerk of the County of Edinburgh. "He is a young shipbuilder," said he, "a son of a shipbuilder, an accomplished draughtsman, and I hear that he lately turned out, from his own design, one of the most perfect ships that ever left Leith Docks; from his childhood upwards he has been an intense student of whatever could be procured concerning the Great Pyramid. His family surname is Menzies."

"This Israelite, then, but no Jew, it was, who first, to my knowledge, broke ground in the Messianic Symbolisms of the Great Pyramid, so intensified subsequently by Mr. Casey, and, after long feeling his way in an humble and prayerful spirit, at length unhesitatingly declared that the immense superiority in height of the Grand Gallery over every other passage in the Great Pyramid, arose from its representing the Christian Dispensation."

"' From the north beginning of the Grand Gallery floor, said Robert Menzies, 'there, in the southward precession, begin the years of the Savior's earthly life, expressed at the rate of a Pyramid inch to a year. Three-and-thirty inch-years, therefore, bring us right over against the mouth of the well, the type of His death, and His glorious resurrection too; while the long, lofty Grand Gallery shows the dominating rule in the world of the blessed religion which He hath established thereby, over-spanned above by the 36 stones of His months of ministry on earth, and defined by the floor-length in inches, (1881 inch years) as to exact periods. The Bible, fully studied, shows that He intended that first dispensation to last only for a time; a time, too, which may terminate very much sooner than most men expect, and shown by the southern wall impending.'"

"Whereupon I went straight to the south wall of the Grand Gallery, and found that it was impending; by the quantity too, if that interests any one, of about one degree, (about six years) and where Mr. Menzies could have got that piece of information from I cannot imagine, for the *north* wall is not impending; he, too, was never at the Great Pyramid, and I have not seen the double circumstance chronicled elsewhere. The first ascending passage, moreover, he explained as representing the Mosaic Dispensation. I measured it, and found it to be, from the north beginning of the Grand Gallery, the natal year of Christ, to its junction with the roof of the entrance-passage northward and below, or to some period in the life of Moses, 1,483 Pyramid inches; and when produced across that passage, so as to touch its floor, 1,542 inches."

"But the chief line of human history with Robert Menzies was the floor of the entrance-passage. Beginning at its upper and northern end, it starts at the rate of a Pyramid inch to a year, from a dispersion of mankind, (2527 B. C.) or from the period when men declined any longer to live the patriarchal life of Divine instruction, and insisted on going off with their own inventions; and which is sensibly represented to the very life or death, in the long-continued descent of the entrance-passage of the Great Pyramid, more than 4,000 inch-years long, until it ends in the Bottomless Pit, a Chamber, already mentioned, deep in the rock. One escape, indeed, there was, in that long and mournful history of human decline; but for a few only, when the exodus took place in the ascending passage, which leads on into the Grand Gallery, showing Hebraism ending in its original prophetic destination—Christianity. But another escape was also eventually provided, to prevent any one being necessarily lost in the bottomless pit; for, before reaching that dismal abyss, there is a possible entrance, though it may be by a strait and narrow way, to the one only gate of salvation through the death of Christ, viz.: the well representing His descent into *hades*, not the bottomless pit of idolaters.

and the wicked at the lowest point to which the entrance passage subterraneously descends, but a natural grotto rather than artificial chamber, in the course of the well's further progress to the other place; while the stone which once covered that well's upper mouth is blown outwards into the Grand Gallery (and was once so thrown out with excessive force, and is now annihilated), carrying part of the wall with it, and indicating how totally unable was the grave to hold Him beyond the appointed time.

"'That sounds fair and looks promising enough, so far,' said Mr. Casey, 'but that is not enough yet to be the turning point with me, when interests so immense are at stake. We must have more than that, and something not less than proof of this order. Measuring along the passages backward from the north beginning of the Grand Gallery, you will find the exodus at either 1483 or 1542 B. C., and the dispersion of mankind in 2527 B. C., up at the beginning of the entrance-passage. Now you have already published, years ago, that you have computed the date of the building of the Great Pyramid, by modern astronomy, based on the Pyramid's own star pointing, and have found it at 2170 B. C. That date, according to this new theory, must be three or four hundred inches down inside the top or mouth of the entrance-passage. Is there any mark at that point? For I feel sure that the builder, if really inspired from on High, would have known how many years were to elapse between his great mechanical work in the beginning of the world, and the one central act of creation in the birth of the Divine Son; and he would have marked it there as the most positive and invaluable proof."

"So away I went," says the Astronomer Royal, "to my original notes to satisfy him, and beginning at the north end of the Grand Gallery, counted and summed up the length of every stone backward all down the first ascending passage, then across the entrance-passage to floor plane towards its mouth, and soon saw that 2170 would fall very near a most singular portion of the passage. This mark was a line ruled on the stone from top to bottom of the passage wall, at right angles to its floor; such a line as might be ruled with a blunt steel instrument, but by a master hand for power and evenness. There was such a line on either wall, the west and the east, of the passage; and the two lines seemed to be pretty accurately opposite to each other. When Mr. Casey required in 1872 to know exactly where, on the floor, the line on either side touched the plane, there was no ready prepared record to say. Every intervening measure by joints between the two extremes, and over scores of joints, had been procured, printed and published to the world in 1867; but just the last item required, merely the small distance from the nearest joint to the drawn line was wanting.

"So I wrote to my friend Mr. Dixon, C. E., then erecting his brother's bridge over the Nile, near Cairo, requesting him to have the goodness to make and send me careful measures of the distance of the fine line on either passage wall at the Pyramid, from the nearest one of the two *quasi*-vertical joints; not giving him any idea what the measure was wanted for, but only asking him to be very precise, clear and accurate. And so he was; taking out also as companion and duplicate measurer, his friend, Dr. Grant, of Cairo;

and their doubly attested figures were sent to me on diagrams, in a manner which left no room for misunderstanding. With this piece of difference measure, I set to work again on my older joint measures of the whole distance; and was almost appalled, when, on applying the above difference, the east side gave forth 2170½, and the west side 2170.14 Pyramid inches, or years.

"'This testimony satisfies me and fills me with thankfulness and joy,' wrote Mr. Casey; 'while I never expected to have measured so closely as that, along either side of those lengthy, dark and sloping Pyramid passages.'"

EXPLANATION OF DIAGRAM

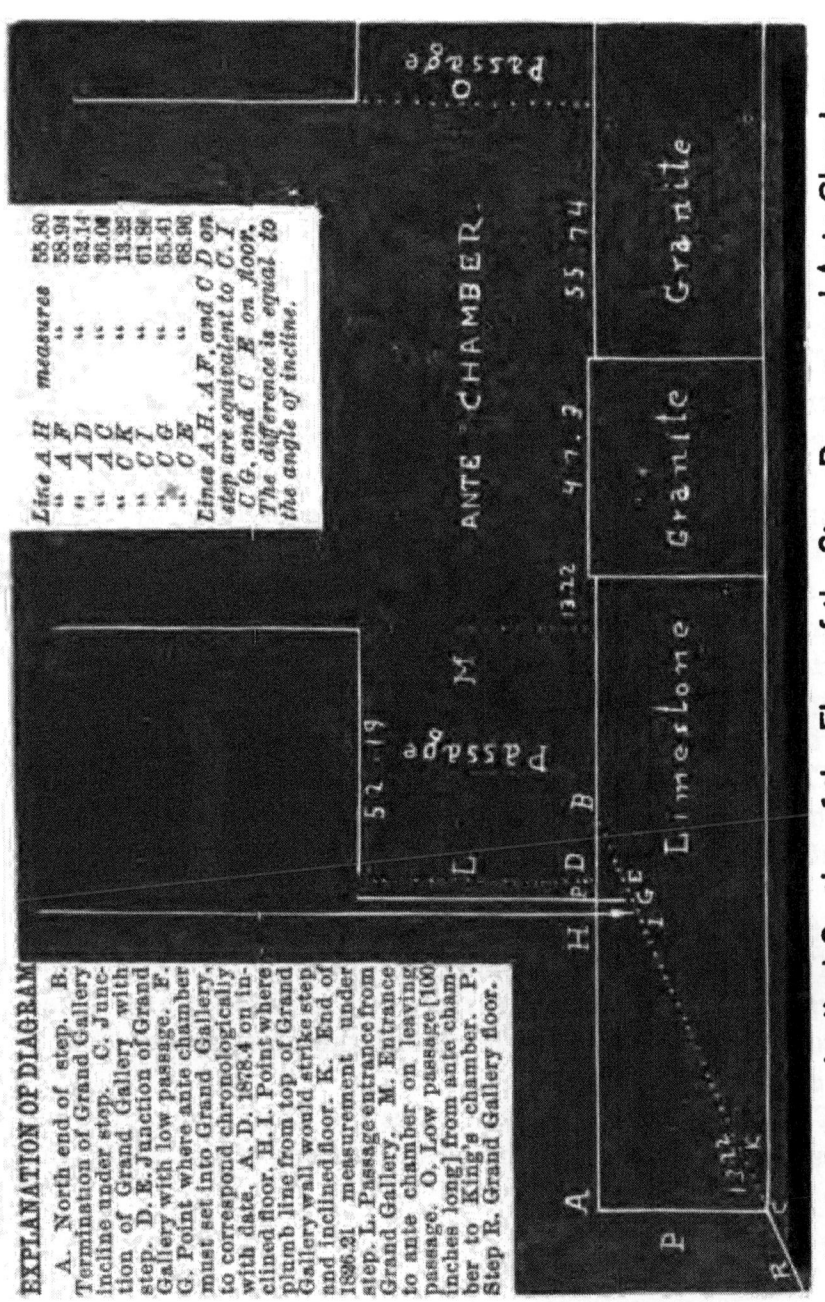

A. North end of step. B. Termination of Grand Gallery incline under step. C. Junction of Grand Gallery with step. D. E. Junction of Grand Gallery with low passage. F. G. Point where ante chamber must set into Grand Gallery, to correspond chronologically with date, A. D. 1878.4 on inclined floor. H. I. Point where plumb line from top of Grand Gallery wall would strike step and inclined floor. K. End of 1890.21 measurement under step. L. Passage entrance from Grand Gallery. M. Entrance to ante chamber on leaving passage. O. Low passage [100 inches long] from ante chamber to King's chamber. P. Step R. Grand Gallery floor.

Line A H	measures	55.80
" A F	"	58.94
" A D	"	62.14
" C K	"	36.08
" C I	"	13.28
" C I	"	61.98
" C G	"	65.41
" C E	"	68.98

Lines A H, A F, and C D on step are equivalent to C. I C.G., and C E on floor. The difference is equal to the angle of incline.

Vertical Longitudinal Section of the Floor of the Step, Passage and Ante-Chamber.

CHAPTER V.

Further Measurements and their Significance.

The length of the Grand Gallery, midway between the floor and roof, is nearly, if not exactly 1878.4 Pyramid inches long. There are, it is known, thirty-six roof stones in this gallery. And there are also seven overlappings of the courses in the side walls. Now 1878.4 divided by the 36 roof stones equals the number of days in a year divided by the seven overlappings on the side walls; or, it equals one year in terms of weeks.

Hence 1878.4 equals the "time" symbolized by the whole length of the Grand Gallery, and probably marks some important event.

The base side length of the Pyramid is 9131.05 Pyramid inches. Divide this by Pyramid number 5, and it equals 1826.21. Call this years, chronologically and beginning at the north end of the Grand Gallery measure that distance south, and it reaches point K beneath the great step.

The length of Grand Gallery to the step (C) is 1812.986 Pyramid inches. Then 1812.21—1812.986=13.224, (diag. C to K) which is also the length of the limestone of floor in ante-chamber.

The next problem demonstrates the thickness of the low passage wall leading to the ante-chamber, at the same time confirming our first date; thus: 1878.4—1826.21= 52.19= thickness of wall as stated.

Prof. Smyth says of the ante-chamber ("L. & W." vol. ii. p. 96) "of the north wall it is of limestone, rough with pick-marks, whilst the other walls are polished. Why is this thus? Mr. Powers says: "Because it is chronologically displaced 55.74 Pyramid inches, south, for the purpose of incorporating and concealing the scientific and spiritual truth therein until the time should come for it to be revealed."

To continue the demonstration, we find that the first granite stone in the floor of the ante-chamber was raised three-tenths of an inch above the limestone preceding and the granite succeeding it, and this too was for a purpose, as we shall see. This raised stone is 47.3 inches long. Then 13.22+47.3=60.52. The whole length of the ante-chamber is 116.26. Then 116.26—60.52=55.74, which is the amount of displacement of the ante-chamber south.

Again, 52.19+13.22=65.41. Then 116.26—65.41=50.85; and —47.3=3.55=distance the ante-chamber must set into the Grand Gallery on the inclined floor to correspond chronologically with the date A. D. 1878.4. Then 55.74—3.55=52.19, or thickness of the wall between the Grand Gallery and ante-chamber.

The distance that the ante-chamber would set in the Grand Gallery being 3.55, if we double this we get 7.10, which is the amount the south wall of the Grand Gallery impends. A plumb line dropped from the top of the Grand Gallery wall would strike the step at point H, and the ante-chamber carried north 55.74 would reach point F. It would also bring the south wall of the ante-chamber flush with the south side of the first granite stone in the ante-chamber floor.

The wall (or passage way) between the ante-chamber and King's Chamber is 100 inches thick. Prof. Smyth has shown that 100 inches is the general Pyramid linear representation of a day of 24 hours. Therefore the King's Chamber chronologically begins 24 hours after the ante-chamber ends.

The north air channel apparently typifies the second coming of Christ. Now when the ante-chamber and King's Chamber are placed in position, as heretofore indicated, then the air channel will enter the King's Chamber direct, and not by a long horizontal passage as now.

In an article entitled "Chronology of the World." by R. Lamb, of Durham, England, published in the "Nation's Glory Leader" of May 2, 1877, he says : "Total from creation of world to birth of Christ, 4104 years. Now if the Christian era commenced in the year of the world 4104, the 6,000 years of the world's history will terminate A. D. 1896."

The Grand Gallery floor line measured from the north end, to the step P at point C=1812.986 inches. This line produced from C to B, computed,=83.1925 ; total, 1896.1785, or Mr. Lamb's date for termination of the 6,000 years.

Mr. W. J. C. Muir says, "The floor line of the Grand Gallery, the grandest feature of the structure in which angle is an element, is the memorial angle of 26° 18', and when produced (C to B) cuts the level of floor of Coffer (King's) Chamber at the East and West *Axial* Plane of the Pyramid."

There is an exceedingly important fact stated in the last

clause of the above sentence, as it determines that point B is exactly in the center of the Pyramid from north to South, on the 50th (Jubilee number) course of masonry.

The measured length of the floor line from the north wall of the Grand Gallery down the first ascending passage to the intersection with entrance passage, thence up to the present north end of the latter=2527.1 inches. Then 2527.1+55.568 (or about the average width of the floor stones) =2582.668, or the "precessional dial" (an important feature in Great Pyramid chronology) divided by ten.

That quantity, 2582.688—2170.5=412.132, the King's Chamber length, and thus Prof. Smyth's measure of 2170.5 on the line mentioned above, to those remarkably drawn lines on the walls of entrance passage, marking the date of the pyramid, is again checked correct, within thirty-six thousandths of an inch ! ! Accurate enough in all good conscience, to satisfy the most fastidious demands of modern exact science.

Again, 2582.668+206.066 (King's Chamber width)= 2788.734, or only 1.266 less than Prof. Smyth's astronomically computed date for the Deluge ; viz.: 2790 B. C.

The precessional dial 25826.78÷25 (inches in sacred cubit) =1033.0672 ; the excess over 1,000 comprising, probably, the exact length of the voluntary life of humiliation in the flesh, of our Savior Jesus the Anointed; or 33 years, 24 days, 13 hours.

The length of ante-chamber 116.26—83.1925 (hypotenuse of step C to B) =33.0675, practically same as above.

33.0672×6=198.4032 equals the time from the death of Jacob (a type of Christ,) to the Exodus from Egypt.

The above facts demonstrate that we have now several very sharply defined points as a basis for chronological calculations, and as the scientific truth embodied in the Pyramid is gradually developed with constantly increasing accuracy in detail, we may expect that the spiritual and chronological truth will be likewise unfolded, in detail as it may please Him who "hath put the times and seasons in His own power," to reveal it to His children. But he who would discover and bring forth the hidden treasures of this great stone-book of revelation and treasure house of truth, must with reverential awe, ever keep in memory this word of the Lord unto Zerubbabel: "Not by might, nor by power, but by my Spirit, saith the Lord of hosts."

The symbolic feature of the Grand Gallery most attractive to travelers, next after its commanding height, is the seven overlappings of its walls. This may be intended to typify the Sabbatical week. Another noticeable feature of the number seven is to be found in the passage leading to the Queen's Chamber. The last part of that passage is found to be nearly one-half greater in depth than the rest; and the length of that deeper part is one-seventh of the whole length of the floor from the beginning of the Grand Gallery up to the Queen's Chamber wall itself. Also, if we take the mean in height of the passage which enters the north end of the Grand Gallery, and of the passage which exits from the south end, we find that that quantity goes seven times exactly to a hundredth, into 339.2, which is the vertical height of the Grand Gallery at a mean of 15 points in its whole length.

There appears to be a certain amount of connection between the Queen's Chamber and the Grand Gallery; for while the Queen's Chamber, with its cubic-defining nich, contains cubic inches to the typical number for that cubit of ten-millionth earth reference, the Grand Gallery contains 36 inclined stones forming its long sloping roof.

There is another calculation that is somewhat singular and seems to connect the Grand Gallery with that New Jerusalem which John saw descending out of heaven. The measure of this city as given in Rev. xxi., 16, was 12,000 furlongs, but the Vatican manuscript reads "twelve times twelve thousand furlongs" which is probably the correct reading inasmuch as it preserves the square of twelve, which is 144; and this number also is given as the height of the wall (144 cubits) and the number of those sealed, (Rev. vii., 4) was 144,000, and the number of those whom John saw standing with the Lamb on Mount Zion was also 144,000. So that the measure of the city is correctly stated at 144,000 furlongs. If we accept the length of a furlong as 250 cubits, then 144,000 × 250 = 36,000,000 cubits. Prof. Smyth tells us that the cubic contents of the Grand Gallery is 36,000,000 inches being one million for each of the 36 stones forming the roof. Let each inch then, represent a cubit, and we have an agreement between the Grand Gallery and the measurement of the New Jerusalem that is remarkable, to say the least. Total contents 36,000,000 ÷ 250 = 144,000.

CHAPTER VI.

The Pyramid's Prophetic Character further Illustrated.

Now the man who built the Great Pyramid, or laid its foundation in 2170 B. C., must have been a contemporary of, but rather older than Abraham, according to the best Biblical Chronology. Melchizedek was a grandly mysterious kingly character, to whom even Abraham offered the tenth of the spoils. He was king of Salem, which some consider to have been Jeru-*salem*.

The Great Pyramid was only to be understood in the latter days of the world, and was destined then to prove the inspiration, origin, and Messianic character of its designs, to both religious and irreligious; in manifesting forth in modes adapted to these and the approaching times, the original and ineffable inspiration of Scripture, — as well as the practical reasons for expecting the return of Christ to an undoubted personal reign for a miraculous season over the entire earth.

"Never was there any building so perfect as the Great Pyramid in fulfilling both the earliest words of the Lord given by Inspiration, and also the New Testament types of the Messiah. And if the Great Pyramid is not mentioned in so clear a manner in the New Testament, that all men may instantly see it, whether by name, or figure, that may arise from its being connected with the second and future rather than with the first and past coming of Christ, which the New Testament was mainly to chronicle and expound. The first ascending passage is found to be 1542 inches long, and these inch years measure the Jewish dispensation, terminating with the first advent at the commencement of the Grand Gallery. Thirty-three inches from the beginning of the Grand Gallery floor is the mouth of a well-like opening descending pretty directly downwards to a cavity in the rock called *Souterrain* below the pyramid base, and then curving southward until it reaches the 4000-inch passage, a little north of the deep subterranean chamber. This well is understood to represent the Savior's death and descent into the grave at the close of His laborious and suffering life of thirty-three years, while the ejection and disruption of the stone that originally closed its mouth expresses His resurrection and triumph.

Following along the Grand Gallery 1815 inches from its commencement brings the explorer to a step which rises about thirty-six inches. Measuring from the step, in the general direction of the ascent, or from 1815 to 1882, are sixty-seven year-inches, but if measured horizontally, along the floor, we have sixty-to sixty-one inches to the wall, or to the commencement of the low passage leading to the antechamber. It is remarkable that the Holy Alliance was formed in 1815, after the terrible wars of France, with an avowed object of creating peace on Christian principles, but really to maintain the existing dynasties. The difference between these two short lengths of sixty-one and sixty-seven inches involves also an interval of difference between 1876 and 1882 inch-years in the entire length, or an interval of six inches. It is a notable circumstance that the southern wall impends over just this space. From 1815 onward we have the day of preparation. This is the period spoken of when many shall run to and fro and knowledge be increased.

The mounting of the step indicates the conquests of Nature's powers in manifold ways. The steamboat, the railroad, and the telegraph, with multitudinous discoveries, all bear witness to this well-defined era. During this period the Word of God has been circulated as never before; during this time there has been developed a marked and decided conviction among the followers of Christ that His advent is imminent. The short difference between the horizontal and slant measures, covered by the impending wall indicates that 1877–1882 will be a very remarkable epoch in human history.

It is a structural fact in the pyramid, that after the Grand Gallery there follows a more contracted passage than any preceding it, running under the impending south wall, and opening into the ante-chamber. The breadth of this south doorway is a little over forty-one inches, and its mean height about forty-three inches. The length of this short passage is fifty-two inches.

Prof. Smyth concludes that this low, difficult, straitened passage, fifty-two inches or years long, must be the period of the times of trouble and perplexity and darkness of the nations, living, not exactly as in the old times, without God in the world, but pretending that they can be a god to themselves by the help of their own science.

To those who think the coming of Christ for His saints is imminent, notwithstanding a period for the duration of those calamities which are to befall the ungodly, may be indicated as above, it may be interesting to quote again from the Astronomer when writing to the editor of a book entitled The Pillar of Witness:

"When the Grand Gallery terminates at the 1881-2 southern end, and a distressingly low passage begins, testifying probably to times of difficulty and oppression to follow, there is a peculiar mode of escape or exit from the upper (or near the ceiling) corner of that southern or 1881-2 end of the Grand Gallery; no less than a small concealed passage-way, far above the heads of all travelers below, and leading to a sort of sanctuary over the ceiling of the King's Chamber, the final end of all the historic series of chambers and passages in the building. This sanctuary is not a place for living human beings, or any walking bodies, the floor being all up and down in huge knobs of granite, and the height too small; but the ceiling of it is exquisitely smooth and true, in polished red granite, and of the same length and breadth as the ceiling of the King's Chamber below.

"There is nothing known in the Egyptological or scientific theories of the Great Pyramid that can pretend to explain that strange exit from the upper corner of the Grand Gallery, twenty-eight feet above its floor, and that one sort of sanctuary to which it leads being thus left accessible to winged beings by the builder; but the sacred theory may point to it as typical of the carrying up of the saints to above the clouds just before the troubles of Antichrist begin.

"There are also four somewhat similar hollows in the masonry above said sanctuary, and they all act with them usefully in defending the King's Chamber from destructive pressure; but the other four are sealed up hollows; why, therefore, was the fifth and lowest one left open and furnished with a regular channel of approach, but one which could not be stormed by the world, or any foot soldiers because it is 28 feet above the floor to which such beings are confined, and is all but invisible from there; in fact I doubt whether one in 500,000 visitors knows anything about it; yet there it is and has been, apparently, from the days of Melchizedek."

The author of the Pillar of Witness says, "We have come to that momentous era to which I have adverted, 1881-2. I do not think the professor expects a positive answer to his question of, 'Why, therefore, was the fifth and lowest one left open and furnished with a regular channel of approach?' for no one from personal observation and prophetic study was better able to reply to it. How interestingly solemn the thought that the only way to escape the unprecedented trouble coming upon this world in the very near future is by that ereptive act by which a prepared and waiting few are caught away to meet the Lord in the air. The same prophet that speaks of the pillar in Egypt foretells the ascent to the safety of the upper courts; 'Come, my people, enter thou into thy chambers and shut thy doors about thee; hide thyself as it were, for a little moment, until the indignation be overpast.'

Mr. Russell, of Canada, says: "My impression regarding

the Grand Gallery would naturally be, that as it commenced with the first advent of Christ, its termination would be with the second advent. Now the question arises, does the Grand Gallery in the Great Pyramid, really and truly represent this dispensation, and does its termination represent the close of the Gospel age referred to by our Lord?

"Looking at the parables recorded in Matt. xiii., we find that they are peculiar to this age, representing its varied progress and sudden and unexpected termination, in the midst of overwhelming judgments upon the wicked, and miraculous escape of the righteous. Now is there anything in the Great Pyramid's Grand Gallery corresponding with what is recorded in those parables, as well as Christ's further prophecy of His second coming, and accompanying events mentioned in Matt. xxiv., Mark xiii., and Luke xxi.? All those prophecies go to show that this gospel age will terminate suddenly and uexpectedly for the great mass of the human race, even as the sudden sweeping deluge in the days of Noah, the elect only escaping, by being gathered by angels from one end of heaven to the other.

"Comparing with the Grand Gallery we find that from the first advent it continues one unbroken passage, ascending uniformly with an incline of 26°, higher and still higher, until it terminates suddenly and abruptly at the south impending wall, where there are but two small passages of exit —one at the bottom of the overhanging wall, a narrow passage or doorway leading down from the level plane of the great step into the ante-chamber, while the other passage of exit leads almost horizontally down from the highest point in the south impending wall, into the heavens above the

King's Chamber. This latter passage can only be approached by persons being caught up,—so the passage may symbolize the coming of Elijah, or the second coming of Christ, or the resurrection of the Bride, the Church of the Firstborn, or it may symbolize all these enumerated events."

After having given his views on the relations sustained by the *Bride*, the *first fruits*, and the *harvest*, to each, Mr. Russell proceeds to inquire:

"What does the passage into the ante-chamber denote? Does it symbolize the great tribulation into which the harvest enters, and is afterwards delivered by entering the ante-chamber? or does the tribulation of the harvest occur this side of the impending wall, and of 1881–2?

"I cannot at present suppose that the north air channel symbolizes the second coming, for then the advent would not take place until we reached the second pilaster in the ante-chamber. According to the New Testament prophecies, Christ comes at the harvest, and the harvest occurs at the end of the age; therefore, if the Grand Gallery represents this dispensation, we can come to no other conclusion, I think, than that Christ is at the very door. One thing is certain: When the Grand Gallery terminates, whatever that may signify, a complete change takes place in the whole course of human events."

Prof. Smyth concludes that the Great Pyramid was built under the influence of Divine inspiration, and that it contains the memorials of a system of weights and measures that are designed to be perpetual, is entitled, at least, to more than ordinary respect and consideration. No less respect is due to the conclusions of the distinguished Astronomer and to the opinions of other talented and learned investigators, that these measures are chronological, and reach great epochs in human history. So far, at least, grand events have occurred where its inch-year periods have indicated marked changes. The 1881–2 inch period, the length of the Grand Gallery, is on the eve of termination. As already stated, there is an egress to a symbolized heavenly chamber of safety, but it is attainable only by beings who can move upward like the angels of God. To do this we must be changed and become like them. A selected company of faithful waiting ones will thus be changed to meet the Lord in the air.

There is another egress, but it leads through a pathway of tribulation. The question now forces itself home upon our attention as to what our own particular, personal destiny shall be. Shall we be left to enter into that time of trouble, such as never was since there was a nation, or shall we escape by a translation? We are entering into the space of those few inch-years covered by the impending wall. The Pyramid indicates the alternative of translation or tribulation.

The Great Pyramid has stood in its solemn, stately grandeur while great empires of the world have arisen, declined and fallen to ruins. Its teachings were only to be understood in the latter days. It now reveals the inspiration, origin, and Messianic character of its designs. Its impressive lesson now is that our dispensation nears its close. About synchronously with the 1881–2 inch termination of the Grand Gallery, we are to have a planetary combination as to three of our largest planets connected with our solar system: In 1880, these planets all reach the nearest point of their several orbits to the sun at precisely the same time in the year. This event has not occurred before for 2,300 years. Let us bear in mind that 2,300 years is the long appointed time given by the "Wonderful numberer" that spans both Jewish and Gentile time. 490 years were cut off on Daniel's people commencing B. C. 420 and ending A. D. 70. The 1,810 years remaining terminates the long vision, when the sanctuary and host shall no longer be trodden under foot. Scientific authority predicts that most wonderful and violent atmospheric and magnetic changes will attend the unusual planetary conjunction. Political changes foretold more than 2,400 years ago are taking place in our present existing generation. A grand crisis is imminent. The whole world is feverish with anxiety. Men's hearts are now failing them for fear and for looking after things that are coming upon the earth. Let us watch, pray, and be sober, and strive to so live that we may at last be found of our Lord in peace, without spot and blameless.

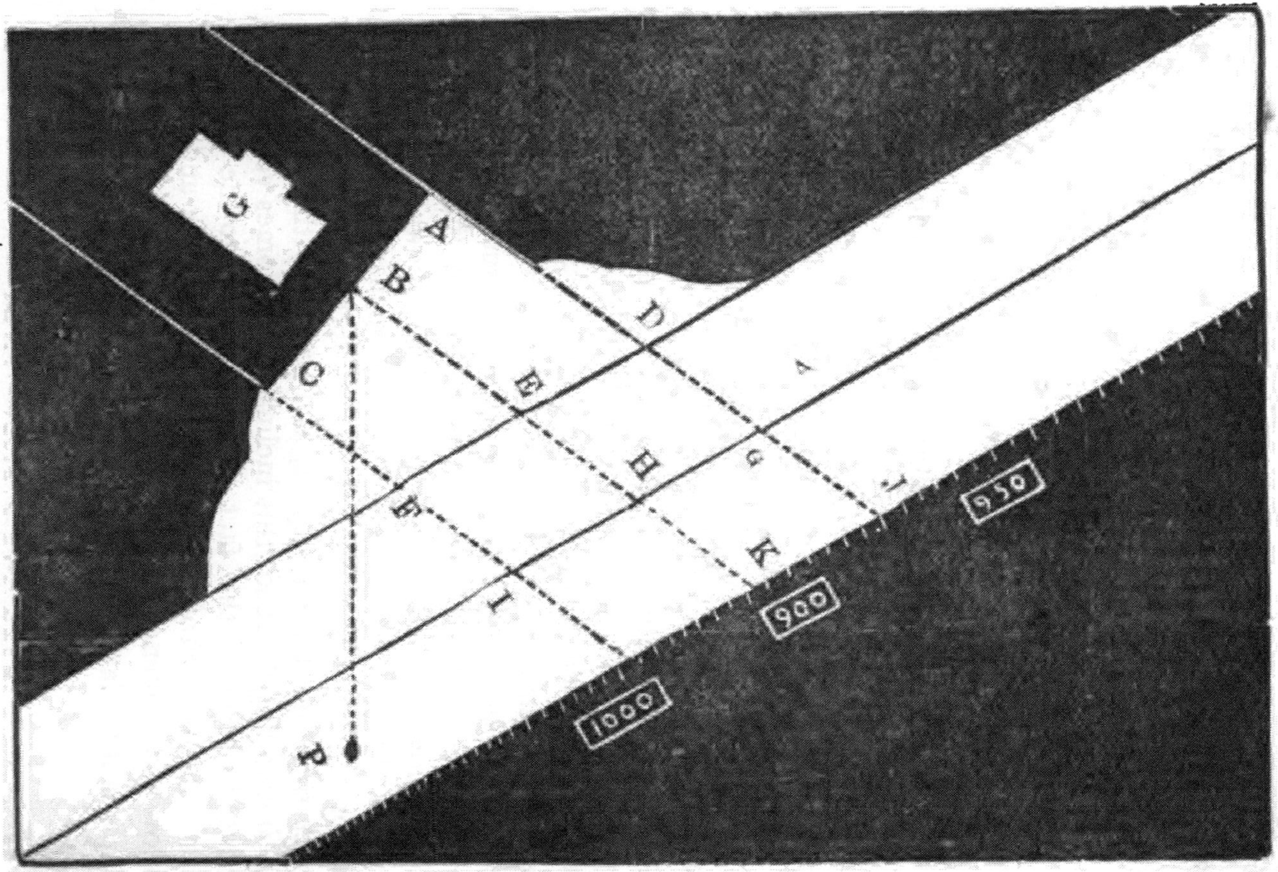
G
A
B
C
D
E
F
H
I
J
K
P
950
900
1000

CHAPTER VIII.

Conclusion.

We have suggested to our minds the grand and intensely interesting fact, that the passage commencing at the opening on the north front of the Great Pyramid, and running south penetrating to the interior of the structure, represents time. Each inch of space along the floor, which the astronomer measured with conscientious and scientific fidelity, is clearly shown to represent a year.

As previously stated, the south wall of the Grand Gallery impends, but what suggested the idea to Robert Menzies that that particular wall should not be perpendicular, is more than we can surmise, in view of the fact that he had never seen the Pyramid. It leans to the north in such a way that a plumb line let down from the top will touch the floor six inches below the wall's base. "The bible shows," says Mr. Menzies, "that God intended this dispensation to last only for a time—and a time which will terminate very much sooner than most men expect, and shown by the southern wall impending." And this inclination becomes very suggestive in view of the fact that according to the careful measurements of Prof. Smyth, 1876 brings us fully under the shadow and influence of that inclination.

How is it to-day? Do not indications already manifest in

the political, social and physical heavens speak of impending change? It is a time of perturbation, not only coming, but already begun, and if indeed commenced, then also how impressively impending! Questions startling and perplexing have arisen, and have assumed an aspect that defies the wisest minds (unaided by revelation) to solve. The sea of society heaves with vast internal commotions. The eye of the statesman sees danger.

The night cometh! Nor does it seem far off. It never appeared so nigh. The shadows are lengthening out and falling with ominous gloom upon the valleys of earth. The dimness of twilight is beginning to make itself felt. It is settling down drearily upon our cities, and on our solitudes; upon the towers of our strength and the palaces of our pomp; nor can the noisy rush of eager multitudes hurrying to and fro for gain or pleasure, wholly stifle the utterance of fear and awe. Men cannot help foreboding evil, for who can tell them what may be in the womb of darkness? The night birds are already on the wing.

Yet it is written also, "the day is at hand!" The night, though dark, will be brief, and will soon be succeeded by a glorious day. But still of that day the night will be the forerunner. And this world's night is surely very near.

Even the potentates of Europe are seemingly strongly impressed with the belief that some extraordinary event is *'impending.'* Pope Pius IX. says, "There is a conflict *'impending'* between the Arch-angel Michael and the Devil;" Disraeli affirms that " there is to be an overturning of the nations, and a great change in the government systems of the world." And other European statesmen are anticipating some great demonstration hitherto not experienced by the inhabitants of earth.

Some thirty years ago when the skies were brighter, men could with comparative safety fold their hands and take their ease. But all this is over. The onward swell of the waters stays not for an hour. There is among the nations a spirit of restlessness, anarchy and insubordination, a passionate love of change, a headlong rush to overturn every established system, too furious and united to be ultimately withstood. The storm, long gathering, but resisted by the barriers which ancients had erected for the stability of kingdoms, is condensing, and overstrained at length will give way to the accumulated pressure. At this crisis the inhabitants of the earth will undoubtedly realize the utter weakness of human efforts and crave Divine assistance, and then will " the Desire of all nations" appear upon the scene and put in operation a train of events which will center in the Holy City, but radiate all over the world, resulting in bringing harmony out of discord, and subjugating all to His sovereign will. What times we are living in truly. How important it is that we should constantly watch, lest the master come and find us unprepared to receive Him. God is represented to our minds as a watchful being, seeing us at all times, noting the fall of an empire as well as a sparrow, seeing our evil and our good. Hence Job says, "For now, thou numberest my steps: dost thou not watch over my sin?" Watching being one of the attributes of the Deity, is certainly for us to follow: hence the frequent command to watch. David prayed, "Set a watch, O Lord, before my mouth; keep the door of my lips." How needful to watch words and deeds lest we fall.

APPENDIX.

The following problems are copied from a pamphlet issued by H. B. Wrey, Rector of Tawstock, Great Britain. The floor of the ante-chamber is partly in granite and partly in limestone, the length of the granite portion being 103.033 inches, and that of the limestone being 13.277, making the whole length of the floor 116.26 pyramid inches. Why these lengths?

I. A square of 103.033 pyramid inches in the side has the same area practically, as a circle of 116.26 inches in its diameter.

II. 103.033 pyramid inches multiplied by 50 gives 5151.65, or is the side of a square of equal area to a triangle of the shape and size of the Great Pyramid's vertical meridian section.

III. 116.26 pyramid inches multiplied by 50 (the ante-chamber standing on the 50th course of masonry), gives 5,813 inches, or the vertical height of the structure.

IV. Taking the granite floor length of the ante-chamber, and using it for a measuring rod in the King's Chamber, we find it goes in the breadth of the floor, exactly twice, and into its length four times, and into its height 2.236 times. This last is an odd number, yet it is the square root of 5, and the sum of the squares of these numbers, that is 4, 16, and 5, is 25, which may be called a Pyramid number.

V. This 103.033 measuring rod will go in the length of a diagonal of the end wall of the King's Chamber exactly three times—into the diagonal of the floor 4.472 times, and into the diagonal of the side wall 4 582. The squares of these numbers are 9, 20, and 21, and their sum is 50, another pyramid number.

VI. This same 103.033 measure is contained in the solid diagonal of the whole King's Chamber, or a line from one corner to the opposite corner, just 5 times, and the square of this is 25.

VII. The sum of these numbers 25, 50 and 25, is 100, and the walls of the King's Chamber, exquisitely constructed in polished red granite in 5 courses, are composed of exactly 100 separate blocks.

THE GREAT PYRAMID. 61

VIII. 412.132 pyramid inches, the length of the King's Chamber, is the diameter in cubits of a circle, whose area equals that of a square, having 365.242 cubits for the length of its side, or one Great Pyramid base side.

IX. A square of 412.132 cubits for the length of one side, is equal in area to a circle whose radius is 232.520 cubits, or the height of the pyramid.

The Great Pyramid is the largest solid building known, its base covering 13½ acres, and the hollow portion of the interior, so far as discovered being only 1.2000 of the whole solid contents. All other pyramids have simply one contracted descending passage, and subterranean cell or cells, while the Great Pyramid has above the base line, ascending passages, and high up in its center, lofty chambers, scientifically and symbolically proportioned. It is also uncontaminated with human egotism, and profane hieroglyphic ornamentation, in a land where pyramids, temples, sarcophagi, etc., almost always teem with idolatrous representations of birds, and beasts, and creeping things.

As to the great question of the sun's distance from the earth, in the age of the Greeks it was fixed at ten miles; is increased slowly to 10,000, yet more slowly to 2,500,000; then after a long delay to 36,000,000, under the German Kelper; to 78,000,000 in the days of Louis XIV., and finally over-passed the true quantity at the beginning of the present century. In view of these facts, how could man unaided, have settled this question in the time of the Great Pyramid? In December, 1874, men of science from every leading nation, were sent all over the world, to observe the Transit of Venus, with the aid of steam navigation, iron ships, electric telegraphs, exquisite telescopes, photographic machines, refined regulator clocks, and chronographs, transit instruments, equatorials, spectroscopes, altitude azimute circles, and all the learning of the universities. What is the result? The English scientists have made no report, pronouncing the computations awfully difficult. But the French have made an adinterim report. *Les Mondes*, in April 1875, says, that M. Puiseux has communicated the first results of the Venus Transit Observations, partly made at the Isle of St. Paul's in the Indian Ocean, and partly made at Pekin, China. The final sum. given for the Solar

Parallax is 8 seconds and 879 thousandths. M. Puiseux says the probable errors will not touch the second fractional figure 7. This, says *Les Mondes*, is equivalent exactly to the set of figures indicated by the GREAT PYRAMID. This astronomic problem was first discovered by Wm. Petrie in 1867, and was represented at the Pyramid 4,000 years ago, by its chief line of measure, or its central vertical height, when multiplied by the numbers which its shape typifies, to wit: 10 raised to the 9th power. In other words, 5819 English inches multiplied by 1,000,000,000=91,840,000 nearly. Well, therefore, may the editor exclaim: "*La Grande Pyramid a vaincu*"—The Great Pyramid has conquered.

The Great Pyramid next teaches the nature of the orbit of the earth around the sun; the exact proportion of the period of that revolution to the rotation of the earth on its axis; the length also of that axis of rotation [500,500,000 British inches]; its expressiveness as a governing symbol for the size and delegated possession of the earth; and typifies the mass of the whole globe, as well as the weight and specific gravity of its solid contents.

Now it may often have excited the surprise of the religious readers of the Bible why the Savior, to such an extent the power and Spirit of God, is so often likened to a "stone."

Yet when those passages are compared and studied, it presently appears that it is by no means an ordinary stone that is alluded to; it is a cut stone—a stone of pointed kind—on which whomsoever falls shall be broken; and of immense size, as well as mounted up at a great height, so that on whomsoever it shall fall, it will grind him to powder; a headstone, moreover, and a topmost corner-stone, so symmetrically completing the whole building it appertains to, that the structure could be no other than a pyramid of the same order as the Great Pyramid—or, rather, it could only be the Great Pyramid itself; and if its head-stone is a favorite Scriptural symbol of Christ, no wonder that Zechariah speaks of the head-stone of the great mountain being brought out with shoutings, crying, "Grace, grace, grace unto it." Or that, when that cornerstone was laid, according to the words of God Himself in Job, "The morningstars sang together, and all the sons of God shouted for joy."

Lightning Source UK Ltd.
Milton Keynes UK
UKHW020154280122
397829UK00007B/1307

9 781375 435697